ESSENTIAL
GUIDE TO KNOWING THE FAITH

●

ETTORE MALNATI

Libreria Editrice Vaticana

United States Conference of Catholic Bishops
Washington, DC

Photos: cover, p. i, Corbis.

First printing, September 2011
ISBN 978-1-60137-146-1

CONTENTS

COMMON PRAYERS

Foreword

he *Catechism of the Catholic Church* is an indispensable instrument for every Christian and every Catholic family. Knowledge of Sacred Scripture, read as the Word of God that nourishes and enlightens, and of the Magisterium of the Church, must be accompanied by the *Catechism*, which presents in a unified and systematic way everything that a Christian must believe in order to live the faith. In the practice of the Catholic Church—this has also been true for the world of the Reformation—after the catechisms that I would call "great," the need has always been felt to publish compendiums, then extracts, and then summaries of the essentials. The reason was to provide outlines of what the Christian is called to know about his or her faith, so that this faith could then be deepened in the various situations or phases of life. This publication, *Essential Guide to Knowing the Faith*, is the result of the pastoral concern of Msgr. Ettore Malnati that Catholic families have at their disposal an easy-to-use resource for approaching those basic notions of the faith, and from there might be "intrigued" into deepening their understanding of them and transmitting them as gift and value in the surroundings and occasions of personal, family, and social life. *Essential Guide to Knowing the Faith* is like a "little catechism," useful on the pastoral level and faithful to Vatican Council II, so that Christian believers may love their faith and give witness to it in truth. I happily endorse the intention of those who asked for this synopsis, extending my encouragement as pastor, so that "Christ may be known, loved, and made known to others."

☩ Giampaolo Crepaldi
Archbishop of Trieste

WHO ARE CHRISTIANS?

ersons who have freely chosen to live Baptism as incorporation into Christ, who has brought them into the Church to be, by their witness, signs in the world of the true identity of the human beings whom God has created and willed in his image and likeness, and whom Christ has made adoptive children of God, offering them a path of salvation in the Church.

Christians are those who set up as the criterion of their life the logic of the Gospel, in observance of the Ten Commandments:

1. I am the LORD your God: you shall not have strange gods before me.
2. You shall not take the name of the LORD your God in vain.
3. Remember to keep holy the LORD's day.

4. Honor your father and your mother.
5. You shall not kill.
6. You shall not commit adultery.
7. You shall not steal.
8. You shall not bear false witness against your neighbor.
9. You shall not covet your neighbor's wife.
10. You shall not covet your neighbor's goods.

Christians know that they cannot, through goodwill alone, come to the faith that is offered to them without their merit, thanks to the work and the person of Christ. Even perseverance as disciples of Christ requires the "work of God" that is the grace offered to the Christian through the "signs of Christ" that are the sacraments consciously celebrated and lived.

Christians are called to live in imitation of Christ, assimilating the theological virtues

of faith, hope, and charity, as well as practic-
ing the cardinal human virtues of prudence,
justice, temperance, and fortitude.

The way of life of the disciples of Christ
is exemplified by the Beatitudes (see Mt
5:3-12):

> Blessed are the poor in spirit,
>   for theirs is the kingdom
>   of heaven.
> Blessed are they who mourn,
>   for they will be comforted.
> Blessed are the meek,
>   for they will inherit the land.
> Blessed are they who hunger and
>   thirst for righteousness,
>   for they will be satisfied.
> Blessed are the merciful,
>   for they will be shown mercy.
> Blessed are the clean of heart,
>   for they will see God.

Blessed are the peacemakers,
  for they will be called children
    of God.
Blessed are they who are persecuted
  for the sake of righteousness,
  for theirs is the kingdom
    of heaven.

Blessed are you when they
insult you and persecute you and
utter every kind of evil against you
[falsely] because of me. Rejoice
and be glad, for your reward will
be great in heaven. Thus they
persecuted the prophets who were
before you.

Christians are those who pray the psalms
with the Liturgy of the Hours, participate
in the weekday Eucharist, and turn to God
every day with the prayer learned from the
Lord Jesus himself:

Our Father who art in heaven,
hallowed be thy name.
Thy kingdom come.
Thy will be done on earth, as it is
    in heaven.
Give us this day our daily bread,
and forgive us our trespasses,
as we forgive those who trespass
    against us,
and lead us not into temptation,
but deliver us from evil. Amen.

For Christians, Sunday is the day of rest, of prayer, and of the Eucharist with the whole community. On this day, God must be clearly in first place for individuals and for the Christian family.

Christians are those who will be recognized by how they love God, not in words but by doing his will and loving their neighbor as themselves.

In What Do Christians Believe?

hey believe

○ In one God, who is in himself a relationship of three persons: Father, Son, and Holy Spirit, equal and distinct, having a single divine substance in common. He is the Omnipotent, the Creator of heaven and earth, the living (*Catechism of the Catholic Church* [CCC], no. 205) and merciful one (CCC, no. 210). Jesus calls him "my Father and your Father."

○ In Christ, the incarnate Word, true God and true man, belonging to the lineage of David, fulfiller of the ancient promises, who suffered under Pontius Pilate, died and was buried, and on the third day rose from the dead

- In the Holy Spirit, the Lord and giver of life, who has spoken through the prophets (CCC, no. 687)
- In the Church, which is one, holy, catholic, and apostolic (CCC, no. 811)
- In the forgiveness of sins (CCC, no. 976)
- In the Communion of Saints
- In the resurrection of the dead at the end of time, and in eternal life (CCC, no. 988)

How Do Christians Behave?

hristians, like all persons, must act justly and in conscience, acquiring the virtues and avoiding sin.

In Conscience

In the intimacy of conscience, human beings discover a law that they do not make for themselves, but that they must obey. In reality, God has written a law within their hearts. Conscience is the most secret core and sanctuary of the human being (CCC, no. 1776). Present in the depths of human beings, the moral conscience enjoins them to do good and avoid evil (CCC, no. 1777). Conscience is a judgment of reason by which persons recognize the moral quality of the actions that they are doing or have done (CCC, no. 1778). The dignity of the person implies and demands rectitude of moral conscience. The conscience must therefore be educated, and moral judgment illuminated. A well-formed conscience is upright and truthful (CCC, no. 1783). Human beings sometimes find themselves facing situations that make moral judgment uncertain. They must always seek what is just and good, and discern the will of God expressed in the divine law (CCC, no. 1787).

Some norms apply in all cases:

○ It is never permitted to do evil so that good may come of it.
○ The golden rule: "Do to others whatever you would have them do to you" (Mt 7:12).
○ Charity always embodies respect of neighbor and of his or her conscience (CCC, no. 1789).

With Virtue

The apostle Paul says: "Whatever is true, whatever is honorable, whatever is just, whatever is pure, whatever is lovely, whatever is gracious, if there is any excellence and if there is anything worthy of praise, think about these things" (Phil 4:8). Christians must seek to acquire both the human and the theological virtues, in that these are a firm, habitual disposition to do good (CCC, no. 1803).

Avoiding Sin

Sin besieges humanity (Heb 12:1). The Christian must cast off its weight (Heb 12:1) following the example of Jesus, the Son of God, who gave his life to save us from sin (see CCC, no. 211). "God is the *Father* Almighty," who "displays his power at its height by freely forgiving sins" (CCC, no. 270).

Angels and men, as intelligent and free creatures, have to journey toward their ultimate destinies by their free choice and preferential love. They can therefore go astray. Indeed, they have sinned. Thus has *moral evil*, incommensurably more harmful than physical evil, entered the world. (CCC, no. 311)

Sin is present in human history. . . . To try to understand what sin is, one must first recognize *the profound relation of man to God*. (CCC, no. 386)

Only the light of divine Revelation clarifies the reality of sin and particularly of the sin committed at mankind's origins. Without the knowledge Revelation gives of God we cannot recognize sin clearly and are tempted to explain it as merely a developmental flaw, a psychological weakness, a mistake, or the necessary consequence of an inadequate social structure, etc. Only in the knowledge of God's plan for man can we grasp that sin is an abuse of the freedom that God gives to created persons so that they are capable of loving him and loving one another. (CCC, no. 387)

The doctrine of original sin, closely connected with that of redemption by Christ, provides lucid discernment of man's situation and activity in the world. . . . Ignorance of the fact that man has a wounded nature inclined to evil gives rise to serious errors in the areas of education, politics, social action, and morals. (CCC, no. 407)

Christians therefore must not only fight against being subjugated to sin and to the structures of sin, they must also build up through their incorporation into Christ, which Baptism offers to them, and through their concrete testimony, a real presence in history so that grace might abound where sin reigned before.

Christians avoid sin not only by their own will, but with the prayer that is communicated to them by "the Spirit of the Son," who "teaches them to pray to the Father and, having become their life, prompts them to act so as to bear 'the fruit of the Spirit'" (CCC, no. 1695), especially through the Sacrament of the Eucharist (CCC, no. 1395).

WHO IS GOD IN CHRISTIAN REVELATION?

 od is love" (1 Jn 4:16). "God is the First and the Last, the beginning and the end of everything" (CCC, no. 198). "There is only one God: 'The Christian faith confesses that God is one in nature, substance, and essence'" (CCC, no. 200). This one God is in three Persons: Father, Son, and Holy Spirit.

> Jesus himself affirms that God is "the one Lord" whom you must love "with all your heart, and with all your soul, and with all your mind, and with all your strength." At the same time Jesus gives us to understand that he himself is "the Lord." To confess that Jesus is Lord is distinctive of Christian faith.

This is not contrary to belief in the One God. Nor does believing in the Holy Spirit as "Lord and giver of life" introduce any division into the One God. . . . "We firmly believe and confess without reservation that there is only one true God, eternal, infinite (*immensus*) and unchangeable, incomprehensible, almighty, and ineffable, the Father and the Son and the Holy Spirit; three persons indeed, but one essence, substance or nature entirely simple." (CCC, no. 202)

The Trinity is One. We do not confess three Gods, but one God in three persons, the "consubstantial Trinity." The divine persons do not share the one divinity among themselves but each of them is God whole and entire: "The Father is that which the Son is, the Son that which the Father is, the Father and the Son that which the Holy Spirit is, i.e., by nature one God." (CCC, no. 253)

The divine Persons are not only names or aspects of the Divine Essence, they "are really distinct from one another. . . . 'He is not the Father who is the Son, nor is the Son he who is the Father, nor is the Holy Spirit he who is the Father or the Son.' They are distinct from one another in their relations of origin" (CCC, no. 254).

"The real distinction of the persons from one another resides solely in the relationships which relate them to one another: 'In the relational names of the persons the Father is related to the Son, the Son to the Father, and the Holy Spirit to both. While they are called three persons in view of their relations, we believe in one nature or substance'" (CCC, no. 255). The God revealed by Jesus Christ is professed by all Christians to be one in three Persons, equal and distinct—Father, Son, and Holy Spirit—and is referred to as the Most Holy Trinity or as the One and Triune God.

WHAT DOES IT MEAN TO BELIEVE IN GOD THE CREATOR?

he catechesis on creation is of capital importance. It means understanding the very foundations of human and Christian life; in fact, the Christian faith provides instructive answers to the fundamental questions that people have asked at every time. From where do we come? Where are we going? What is our origin? What is our end? (see CCC, no. 282).

The question of the origins of the world and of humanity is the object of many scientific studies that have greatly expanded our understanding of the age and dimensions of the cosmos, the development of life forms, the appearance of the human species.

These scientific discoveries invite us to an ever greater admiration for the greatness of the Creator, and to thank him for all his works (see CCC, no. 283).

Undoubtedly, human intelligence can find its own answer to the problem of origins. In fact, it is possible to know with certainty that God the Creator exists, through his works (see CCC, no. 286). Beyond the natural understanding that every human being can have of the Creator, God progressively revealed to the People of Abraham the mystery of creation (see CCC, no. 287).

The revelation of creation is inseparable from the revelation and realization of the Covenant of the one God with his People (see CCC, no. 288).

We believe that God created the world according to his wisdom (see CCC, no. 295), and that he created it freely and from nothing (see CCC, no. 296). Faith in creation from nothing is attested to by Scripture as a truth full of promise and hope (see CCC, no. 297).

Because God creates according to wisdom, creation has an order. Created in the eternal Word, it is destined for human beings and entrusted to them as a gift (see CCC, no. 299).

> Creation has its own goodness and proper perfection, but it did not spring forth complete from the hands of the Creator. The universe was created "in a state of journeying" (*in statu viae*) toward an ultimate perfection yet to be attained. (CCC, no. 302)

> God does not abandon his creatures to themselves. (CCC, no. 301)

The Apostolic Symbol professes that God is the Creator of heaven and earth, meaning of all things visible and invisible (see CCC, no. 325), "the spiritual and the corporeal, that is, the angelic and the earthly, and then, the human creature, who as it were shares in both orders, being composed of spirit and body" (CCC, no. 327).

> The existence of the spiritual, non-corporeal beings that Sacred Scripture usually calls "angels" is a truth of faith. (CCC, no. 328)

> As purely *spiritual* creatures angels have intelligence and will: they are personal and immortal creatures, surpassing in perfection all visible creatures (CCC, no. 330).

> Scripture speaks of a sin of these angels. This "fall" consists in the free choice of these created spirits, who radically and irrevocably *rejected* God and his reign. (CCC, no. 392)

These rebel angels are referred to as demons or devils.

Their sin cannot be forgiven, since their free choice is irrevocable in nature (see CCC, no. 393).

Divine permission of diabolical activity is a great mystery (see CCC, no. 394).

CAN HUMAN BEINGS KNOW GOD BY REASON ALONE?

uman beings can know God through the gift of natural reason (see CCC, no. 36), but under actual conditions they encounter many difficulties in knowing God by reason alone (see CCC, no. 37), so they need to be enlightened by Revelation (see CCC, no. 38).

In fact, "the desire for God is written in the human heart, because man is created by God and for God; and God never ceases to draw man to himself. Only in God will he find the truth and happiness he never stops searching for" (CCC, no. 27).

> In many ways, throughout history down to the present day, men have given expression to their quest for

God in their religious beliefs and behavior: in their prayers, sacrifices, rituals, meditations, and so forth. These forms of religious expression, despite the ambiguities they often bring with them, are so universal that one may well call man a *religious being*. (CCC, no. 28)

The person who seeks God through reason discovers some ways of arriving at knowledge of him. These are also called proofs of the existence of God, not in the sense of the proofs that are sought in the field of the natural sciences, but in the sense of converging and convincing arguments that allow one to reach real certainties. The starting point of these ways to approach God is creation: the material world and the human person (see CCC, no. 31).

The World

Starting from the movement, becoming, contingency, order, and beauty of the world, one can come to know God as the origin and end of the universe. In regard to the pagans, St. Paul affirms: "For what can be known about God is evident to them, because God made it evident to them. Ever since the creation of the world, his invisible attributes of eternal power and divinity have been able to be understood and perceived in what he has made" (Rom 1:19-20). And St. Augustine: "Question the beauty of the earth, question the beauty of the sea, question the beauty of the air, amply spread around everywhere, question the beauty of the sky . . . question all these things. They all answer you, 'Here we are, look; we're beautiful.' Their beauty is their confession. Who made these beautiful changeable things, if not one who is beautiful and unchangeable?" (*Sermones*, 241, 2).[1]

---

1   *www.vatican.va/spirit/documents/spirit_20000721_agostino_en.html*

Human Beings

With their openness to truth and goodness, with their sense of moral good and evil, with their freedom and voice of conscience, with their yearning for the infinite and for happiness, human beings wonder about the existence of God. In these openings, they perceive signs of their own spiritual souls. Bearing "the seed of eternity, which cannot be reduced to sheer matter" (*Gaudium et Spes*, no. 18, see no. 14), their souls can have their origin in only one God.

The world and human beings attest that they do not have in themselves either their first principle or their ultimate end, but that they participate in absolute Being, which does not have either an origin or an end. Thus, through these various "ways," human beings can come to knowledge of the existence of a reality that is the first cause and the ultimate end of everything, and "that everyone calls 'God'" (St. Thomas Aquinas,

Summa Theologiae, I, 2, 3, quoted in CCC, no. 34). Human beings have a faculty that makes them capable of knowing the existence of a personal God. But in order that human beings might enter into intimacy with him, God has willed to reveal himself and give them the grace to receive this revelation in faith. Nonetheless, the "proofs" of the existence of God can prepare the way for faith and help to show that faith is not opposed to human reason (see CCC, nos. 32-35).

WHO IS CHRIST JESUS?

hrist Jesus is the Word of God made man while still remaining true God (see CCC, no. 464). In the one person of the incarnate Word are both the human and the divine natures. Precisely because of this identity, he wanted and was able to save and redeem all humanity. The human soul that the Word of God has assumed is endowed with true human knowledge (see CCC, no. 472). Christ Jesus has two wills and two operations: divine and human, not in opposition, but in cooperation. The human will of Christ follows the divine will, without opposition (see CCC, no. 475).

Jesus Christ was conceived by the work of the Holy Spirit in the womb of the Virgin Mary (see CCC, no. 504), who in this way cooperated in the salvation of humanity with free faith and obedience (see CCC, no. 511). Jesus began his public life with his Baptism by John in the Jordan (see CCC, no. 535). By submitting to this Baptism, Jesus accepted and inaugurated his mission as the Suffering Servant (see CCC, no. 536).

After John the Baptist was arrested, Christ Jesus began to proclaim the Gospel, beginning in Galilee, and, fulfilling the will of the Father, inaugurated the Kingdom of heaven (see CCC, no. 541) into which all human beings are called to enter (see CCC, no. 543).

From the beginning of his public life, Jesus chose twelve men to be with him and take part in his mission (see CCC, no. 552). In the college of the Twelve, Simon Peter occupies the first place (see CCC, no. 552).

Jesus, preceded and accompanied by the Twelve, went from village to village in Galilee, Samaria, and Judea, proclaiming the Gospel. "When the days for his being taken up were fulfilled, he resolutely determined to journey to Jerusalem" (Lk 9:51), expressing his willingness to offer up his life.

The entry of Jesus into Jerusalem manifests the advent of the Kingdom that the King-Messiah is preparing to realize with the Passover of his Death and Resurrection (see CCC, no. 560).

Jesus' violent death was not the result of chance; it belongs to the mystery of the divine plan (see CCC, no. 599). This is what Peter told the Jews in Jerusalem: "This man [was] delivered up by the set plan and foreknowledge of God" (Acts 2:23). The redemptive death of Jesus fulfills the prophecy of the suffering servant (Is 53:7-8). It was Jesus himself, after the Resurrection, who gave this interpretation to the disciples in Emmaus (see CCC, no. 601). The free offering of Christ Jesus on the Cross to take away the sin of the world (see CCC, no. 608) was anticipated at the Last Supper (see CCC, no. 610) when he, on the eve of his Passion, made that "Passover banquet" the memorial of his voluntary offering of himself to the Father for the salvation of humanity: "This is my blood of the covenant, which will be shed on behalf of many for the forgiveness of sins" (Mt. 26:28; see CCC, no. 610). After the sacrifice on the Cross, Christ with his soul united with his divine Person descended to the dwelling of the dead. He thus opened the doors of heaven to the just people who had gone before him (see CCC, no. 637). Risen, he manifested himself to his disciples gathered in the upper room and offered his peace, as well as the power to forgive sins. The Resurrection of Jesus was not a return to earthly life like his raising of Lazarus before the Passover. This Resurrection is fundamentally different. In his risen body, he passes from death to another life beyond time and space. He, as the apostle Paul says, is the man of heaven (see CCC, no. 646). "If Christ has not been raised, then empty [too] is . . . your faith" (1 Cor 15:14). He ascended to the Father (see CCC, no. 663), and this marks the definitive entry of the humanity of Jesus into the heavenly Kingdom of God (see CCC, no. 665), from where on the day of judgment, at the end of the world, he will come in glory to achieve the definitive triumph of good over evil (see CCC, no. 681) and to judge the living and the dead.

HOW CAN WE BENEFIT FROM THE WORK OF CHRIST?

e can benefit from the work of Christ through the sacraments, signs that he instituted and ordained for the sanctification of humanity and for building up the Body of Christ, the Church (see CCC, no. 1123). There are seven sacraments in the Church: Baptism, Confirmation or Chrismation, the Eucharist, Penance, the Anointing of the Sick, Holy Orders, and Matrimony (CCC, no. 1113), all of them instituted by Christ our Lord (see CCC, no. 1114). The sacraments, celebrated worthily in faith, confer the grace that they signify. They are efficacious because Christ himself acts in them (see CCC, no. 1127).

The Church celebrates the sacraments as a priestly community structured through the baptismal priesthood and that of the ordained ministers (see CCC, no. 1132). The Seven Sacraments touch on all the stages and moments of Christian life (see CCC, no. 1210) and are subdivided (see CCC, no. 1211) into

○ Sacraments of Christian Initiation (Baptism, Confirmation, Eucharist)
○ Sacraments of Healing (Penance and Anointing of the Sick)
○ Sacraments of Communion and Mission (Holy Orders and Matrimony)

In addition to being the "door," as St. Ambrose says, that allows us into the Church, Baptism is necessary because it erases the Original Sin contracted by humanity with the sin of Adam that impoverished it. Thanks to the merits of Christ, who offers the gift of justification to those who receive it, the Christian is "called to share in the life of the Blessed Trinity, here on earth in the obscurity of faith, and after death in eternal light" (see CCC, no. 265).

The Sacraments of Confirmation, Eucharist, Holy Orders, and Matrimony must be received in the grace of God. Baptism, Confirmation, and Holy Orders confer the character that is the seal with which the Holy Spirit has marked us "for the day of redemption" (Eph 4:30). The believer who has kept the seal to the end will be able to die marked with the sign of faith (see CCC, no. 1274).

In the sacramental order, a unique and singular place belongs to the Eucharist, which is the Sacrament of sacraments, in that all the others are ordered to it as their specific end (see CCC, no. 1211).

The Eucharist is the memorial of the Passover of Christ, of the work of salvation achieved through the life, Death, and Resurrection of Christ, a work that is made present in the liturgical action (see CCC, no. 1409). It is Christ himself, the High and Eternal Priest of the New Covenant, who, acting through the ministry of the priests, offers the eucharistic sacrifice. And Christ himself, really present under the species of bread and wine, is also the offering of the eucharistic sacrifice (see CCC, no. 1410).

Receiving the Eucharist in Communion has as its principal fruit an intimate union with Christ Jesus (CCC, no. 1391). It separates us from sin (see CCC, no. 1393), unites us in a closer bond with Christ (CCC, no. 1395), and is a pledge of future glory (see CCC, no. 1402).

WHAT IS THE CHURCH?

he Church is the People of the New Covenant willed by Christ Jesus to be his mystical Body in the world. It is one, holy, catholic, and apostolic, precisely in its profound and ultimate identity (CCC, no. 865).

The Church is one because of its founder, Christ Jesus, because of its soul, the Holy Spirit (see CCC, no. 813). From its beginning, this "one" Church nevertheless presents great diversity that comes both from the variety of God's gifts and from the multiplicity of persons who receive it (see CCC, no. 814). The unity of the Church in time is also guaranteed by visible bonds of communion:

○ The profession of a single faith received from the apostles

○ The common celebration of divine worship, especially of the sacraments

○ The apostolic succession through the Sacrament of Holy Orders (see CCC, no. 815)

We believe that the unity that Christ has given to his Church from the beginning subsists in the Catholic Church (see CCC, no. 820).

The Church is holy in that, being united with Christ, it is sanctified by him and through him becomes sanctifying itself (see CCC, no. 824). Already on the earth, the Church is adorned with a real, though imperfect, holiness. In its members, this holiness must be achieved (see CCC, no. 825). While Christ did not know sin, but made himself sin to redeem those who have sinned, the Church, which clasps sinners to its bosom although it is holy, in that it is united with Christ, is at the same time in need of purification (see CCC, no. 827). We affirm with Paul VI that the Church is holy although it clasps sinners to its bosom, since it possesses no life other than that of grace (see *Credo of the People of God*, 1968).

The Church is catholic in a twofold sense:

○ Because Christ is present in it, and the fullness of the Body of Christ united with its Head subsists in it. This implies that it receives from him in a full and total form the means of salvation that Christ has willed (see CCC, no. 830).
○ Because it has been sent on mission by Christ to the totality of the human race (see CCC, no. 831), as we learn from the Risen Lord himself: "Go, therefore, and make disciples of all nations, baptizing them in the name of the Father, and of the Son, and of the holy Spirit, teaching them to observe all that I have commanded you" (Mt 28:19-20).

The protagonist of the Church's mission is the Holy Spirit. Under the influence of the Holy Spirit, the Church must proceed along the same path followed by Jesus (see CCC, no. 852). The Church's mission requires an effort toward Christian unity (see CCC, no. 855) and implies a respectful dialogue with those who do not yet accept the Gospel (see CCC, no. 856).

The Church is apostolic

○ Because it is founded on the Apostles, witnesses chosen and sent on mission by Christ to preserve the *depositum fidei* and transmit the teaching given to the Apostles by Jesus

○ Because until the glorious return of Christ in his Parousia, it continues to be instructed and guided by the Apostles thanks to their successors in their pastoral mission: the college of bishops, assisted by the presbyters and united with the successor of Peter (see CCC, no. 857).

The whole Church is apostolic in that it remains in a communion of faith and life with its origin through the successors of Peter and of the Apostles.

The whole Church is apostolic in that it is sent to the entire world; all of its members, by virtue of Baptism, although in different ways, participate in this mission (see CCC, no. 863).

One becomes part of the Church through response and adherence to the proclamation of the Gospel and through Baptism, both for adults and for children, whose faith and decision are guaranteed by their parents and by the Church itself. "In virtue of their rebirth in Christ there exists among all the Christian faithful a true equality with regard to dignity and the activity whereby all cooperate in the building up of the Body of Christ in accord with each one's own condition and function" (CCC, no. 872).

> The very differences which the Lord has willed to put between the members of his body serve its unity and

mission. . . . "To the apostles and their successors Christ has entrusted the office of teaching, sanctifying, and governing in his name and by his power. But the laity are made to share in the priestly, prophetical, and kingly office of Christ; they have therefore, in the Church and in the world, their own assignment in the mission of the whole People of God." Finally, "from both groups [hierarchy and laity] there exist Christian faithful who are consecrated to God in their own special manner and serve the salvific mission of the Church through the profession of the evangelical counsels." (CCC, no. 873)

When Christ instituted the Twelve, "he constituted [them] in the form of a college or permanent assembly, at the head of which he placed Peter." (CCC, no. 880)

"The Lord made Simon alone, whom he named Peter, the 'rock' of his Church. He gave him the keys of his Church and instituted him shepherd of the whole flock" (CCC, no. 881) and asked him to confirm his fellow believers in the faith. This pastoral office of Peter "continues" in his successor, the Bishop of Rome, as "the perpetual and visible source and foundation of the unity both of the bishops and of the whole company of the faithful" (CCC, no. 882).

WHO IS THE HUMAN PERSON?

he human person is created by God in his image and likeness, male and female he created them (Gn 1:27). Of all the visible creatures, only human beings are capable of knowing and loving their own Creator. Only the human person is called to share, in knowledge and love, the life of God (see CCC, no. 356). Being in the image of God, the human being has the dignity of a person (see CCC, no. 357). God has created everything for the human person, but the human person was created to serve and love God (see CCC, no. 358) in this life and to enjoy him in the next.

The human person, created in the image of God, is both a corporeal and spiritual being (see CCC, no. 362), formed of soul and body. The unity of soul and body is so profound that the soul must be considered the form of the body (see CCC, no. 365). The Church teaches that every spiritual soul is directly created by God—it is not produced by the parents—and is immortal (see CCC, no. 366).

Man and woman are created by God in perfect equality. Man and woman are like an identical unit in the image of God (see CCC, no. 369). Created together, man and woman are willed by God for one another (see CCC, nos. 371-372). In the plan of God, man and woman are called to rule the earth as God's stewards (see CCC, no. 373).

According to the biblical narrative, the progenitors of humanity, Adam and Eve, were constituted in a state of original holiness and justice (see CCC, no. 376). Because of the original sin committed by the progenitors, all of the harmony of the original justice that God, in his plan, had foreseen for them would be lost (see CCC, no. 379).

The biblical account of the fall of the progenitors (Gn 3) uses a language of images but expresses a primordial event, an event that happened at the beginning of human history. Revelation gives us the certainty of faith that all of human history is marked by the original fault committed freely by our progenitors (see CCC, no. 390). With this sin, human beings preferred themselves to God, pitting themselves against God (see CCC, no. 398). The consequences of this are that Adam and Eve immediately lose the grace of original holiness. They are afraid of God (see CCC, no. 399).

The harmony in which they were created is destroyed; the command of the spiritual faculties over the body is shattered; the union of man and woman is subjected to tensions; their relationship will be marked by concupiscence and by the tendency to subjugation. Harmony with creation is broken. Because of human beings, creation is subjected to the slavery of corruption. Human beings will return to dust. Death, with its anguish, enters into the history of humanity (see CCC, no. 400). Although the original fault was committed as a personal sin by the progenitors alone (f. CCC, no. 405), it is transmitted to all of humanity and to each person (see CCC, no. 404) with the human nature, not by imitation, but by propagation, an inclination that is "called 'concupiscence'" (CCC, no. 418). This sin, which Christ took away through his obedience to the Father, is erased by the Baptism that the Church, on the command of the Risen One, also administers to children (see CCC, no. 403).

Human beings are mortal, and therefore conclude their earthly experience with death. For the Christian, this is not the end, but the passage into eternal life. "The Church encourages us to prepare ourselves for the hour of our death" (CCC, no. 1014).

> In death, God calls man to himself. (CCC, no. 1011)

Each man receives his eternal retribution in his immortal soul at the very moment of his death, in a particular judgment that refers his life to Christ: either entrance into the blessedness of heaven—through a purification or immediately,—or immediate and everlasting damnation. "At the evening of life, we shall be judged on our love." (CCC, no. 1022)

At the end of time, with the Parousia of Christ and the universal judgment, "God, in his almighty power, will definitively grant incorruptible life to our bodies by reuniting them with our souls, through the power of Jesus' Resurrection" (CCC, no. 997).

For man, this consummation will be the final realization of the unity of the human race, which God willed from creation and of which the pilgrim Church has been "in the nature of sacrament." Those who are united with

Christ will form the community of the redeemed, "the holy city" of God, "the Bride, the wife of the Lamb." (CCC, no. 1045)

WHAT IS CHRISTIAN PRAYER?

rayer is *Christian* insofar as it is communion with Christ and extends throughout the Church, which is his Body. Its dimensions are those of Christ's love" (CCC, no. 2565).

> The Christian begins his day, his prayers, and his activities with the Sign of the Cross: "in the name of the Father and of the Son and of the Holy Spirit. Amen." (CCC, no. 2157)
>
> Christian prayer is a covenant relationship between God and man in Christ. It is the action of God and of man, springing forth from both the Holy Spirit and ourselves, wholly directed to the Father, in union with

the human will of the Son of God made man. (CCC, no. 2564)

Christ Jesus himself "often draws apart to pray *in solitude*, on a mountain, preferably at night. *He includes all men in his prayer*" (CCC, no. 2602). "The Gospel also gives us Jesus' explicit teaching on prayer. Like a wise teacher he takes hold of us where we are and leads us progressively toward the Father" (CCC, no. 2607).

Three parables on prayer have been handed down to us by the evangelist Luke: Lk 11:5-3; Lk 18:1-8; Lk 18:9-14.

> When Jesus openly entrusts to his disciples the mystery of prayer to the Father, he reveals to them what their prayer and ours must be. . . . What is new is to "ask *in his name.*" (CCC, no. 2614)

> In the first place these are prayers that the faithful hear and read in the

Scriptures, but also that they make their own—especially those of the Psalms, in view of their fulfillment in Christ. (CCC, no. 2625)

In prayer, the pilgrim Church is associated with that of the saints, whose intercession she asks. (CCC, no. 2692)

The Christian family is the first place for education in prayer. (CCC, no. 2694)

The most appropriate places for prayer are personal or family oratories, monasteries, places of pilgrimage, and above all the church, which is the proper place for liturgical prayer for the parish community and the privileged place for Eucharistic adoration. (CCC, no. 2696)

The Church invites the faithful to regular prayer: daily prayers, the Liturgy of the Hours, Sunday Eucharist, the feasts of the liturgical year. (CCC, no. 2720)

The Christian tradition comprises three major expressions of the life of prayer: vocal prayer, meditation, and contemplative prayer. They have in common the recollection of the heart. (CCC, no. 2721).

Prayer and *Christian life* are *inseparable*, for they concern the same love and the same renunciation, proceeding from love. . . . "He 'prays without ceasing' who unites prayer to works and good works to prayer. Only in this way can we consider as realizable the principle of praying without ceasing." (CCC, no. 2745)

WHY THE DIALOGUE BETWEEN THE CHURCH AND OTHER RELIGIONS?

ecause those who have not yet received the Gospel are connected to the People of God in various ways (see CCC, no. 839). The Church is in relation with all religions because it recognizes in them the search, still in shadows and images, of a God unknown but near (see CCC, no. 843), and in particular

- ○ With the Jewish religion, recognizing in the People of Abraham the first People among all humanity to receive the Word, and in the Jewish faith the first response to the Revelation of God in the Old Testament (see CCC, no. 839)
- ○ With the Muslims, in that the plan of salvation also embraces those who

recognize the Creator, and this also includes the Muslims, who profess to have their faith from Abraham and with us worship one merciful God who will judge humanity on the last day (see CCC, no. 841)

- ○ With all believers in God, in that "the Catholic Church recognizes in other religions that search, among shadows and images, for the God who is unknown yet near. . . . The Church considers all goodness and truth found in these religions as 'a preparation for the Gospel'" (CCC, no. 843).

COMMON PRAYERS

Sign of the Cross

In the name of the Father
and of the Son
and of the Holy Spirit. Amen.

Glory Be (Doxology)

Glory be to the Father
and to the Son
and to the Holy Spirit,
as it was in the beginning
is now, and ever shall be
world without end. Amen.

Hail Mary

Hail, Mary, full of grace,
the Lord is with thee.
Blessed art thou among women
and blessed is the fruit of thy womb, Jesus.
Holy Mary, Mother of God,
pray for us sinners,
now and at the hour of our death. Amen.

Prayer to One's Guardian Angel

Angel of God, my guardian dear,
to whom God's love commits me here,
ever this day be at my side,
to light and guard, to rule and guide.
   Amen.

Prayer for the Souls in Purgatory

Eternal rest grant unto them, O Lord,
    and let perpetual light shine upon them.
May the souls of all the faithful departed,
    through the mercy of God, rest in
    peace. Amen.

Angelus

V. The Angel of the Lord declared unto
    Mary.
R. And she conceived of the Holy Spirit.

Hail, Mary, full of grace,
the Lord is with thee.
Blessed art thou among women
and blessed is the fruit of thy womb, Jesus.
Holy Mary, Mother of God,
pray for us sinners,
now and at the hour of our death. Amen.

V. Behold the handmaid of the Lord.
R. Be it done unto me according to
   thy word.
Hail Mary.

V. And the Word was made flesh.
R. And dwelt among us.
Hail Mary.

V. Pray for us, O holy Mother of God.
R. That we may be made worthy of the
   promises of Christ.

Let us pray:
Pour forth, we beseech thee, O Lord, thy
grace into our hearts; that we, to whom
the Incarnation of Christ, thy Son, was
made known by the message of an angel,
may by his Passion and Cross be brought
to the glory of his Resurrection. Through
the same Christ, our Lord. Amen.

Queen of Heaven (*Regina Caeli*)

Queen of heaven, rejoice, alleluia.
The Son whom you merited to bear,
    alleluia,
has risen as he said, alleluia.
Pray for us to God, alleluia.
Rejoice and be glad, O Virgin Mary,
    alleluia!
For the Lord has truly risen, alleluia.

Let us pray:
O God, who through the resurrection
of your Son, our Lord Jesus Christ, did
vouchsafe to give joy to the world; grant,
we beseech you, that through his Mother,
the Virgin Mary, we may obtain the joys
of everlasting life. Through the same
Christ our Lord. Amen.

Hail, Holy Queen

Hail, Holy Queen, Mother of Mercy,
our life, our sweetness and our hope.
To thee do we cry,
poor banished children of Eve.
To thee do we send up our sighs,
mourning and weeping in this valley
    of tears.
Turn then, most gracious advocate,
thine eyes of mercy toward us,
and after this our exile
show unto us the blessed fruit of thy
    womb, Jesus.
O clement, O loving,
O sweet Virgin Mary.

Memorare

Remember, O most gracious Virgin Mary, that never was it known that anyone who fled to thy protection, implored thy help, or sought thy intercession, was left unaided. Inspired by this confidence I fly unto thee, O Virgin of virgins, my Mother. To thee do I come, before thee I stand, sinful and sorrowful. O Mother of the Word Incarnate, despise not my petitions, but in thy mercy hear and answer me. Amen.

Act of Faith

O my God, I firmly believe that you are one God in three divine Persons, Father, Son, and Holy Spirit. I believe that your divine Son became man and died for our sins and that he will come to judge the living and the dead. I believe these and all the truths which the Holy Catholic

Church teaches because you have revealed them who are eternal truth and wisdom, who can neither deceive nor be deceived. In this faith I intend to live and die. Amen.

Act of Hope

O Lord God, I hope by your grace for the pardon of all my sins and after life here to gain eternal happiness because you have promised it who are infinitely powerful, faithful, kind, and merciful. In this hope I intend to live and die. Amen.

Act of Love

O Lord God, I love you above all things and I love my neighbor for your sake because you are the highest, infinite and perfect good, worthy of all my love. In this love I intend to live and die. Amen.

Act of Contrition

O my God, I am heartily sorry for having offended Thee, and I detest all my sins because of thy just punishments, but most of all because they offend Thee, my God, who art all good and deserving of all my love. I firmly resolve with the help of Thy grace to sin no more and to avoid the near occasion of sin. Amen.

ABOUT THE AUTHOR

ttore Malnati is a professor of human rights at the faculty of political science of the University of Trieste, where he also taught peace studies while studying for his degree in diplomatic sciences. He also teaches at the Theological Faculty of Lugano, at the inter-diocesan institute of Friuli-Venezia Giulia, and at other higher institutes of religious studies. The author of numerous publications, he is also the president of the cultural association Studium Fidei in Trieste, and has been a member of the Russian Academy of Natural Sciences since 2000.

With the LEV, he published a commentary on the Apostolic Exhortation *Marialis Cultus* in 2004, and a commentary on *Caritas in Veritate* in 2009.